DISCOVER YOUR MOJO

SECRETS TO UNRAVELLING YOUR UNIQUE MAGICAL CHARM!

RINNKU. G

Made with ❤ on the Notion Press Platform
www.notionpress.com

Contents

Prologue

I spent 37 years of my life mechanically, doing what everyone does, study, work, cook, look after family, and do what everyone considers good to do. I consider myself to be an optimist, someone with a never say die spirit and one who keeps moving forward no matter what the obstacles are. I am also an enthusiastic learner and a big book worm. My biggest lessons have come from observation and my life experiences. As a child my teachers would say that a human being uses only 10% of the mind potential, imagine what one could achieve if we used the rest of the 90%. Hence, the workings of the mind, why people behave the way they do, why some are happy and successful, and others are not, such questions kept bothering me. I attended seminars, learnt from a lot of gurus, from nature around me and from everything that happened to me. This book is what I discovered and learnt. This book is all my mantras, my secrets to moving from one a one room rented house to buying my own house at the age of 27, from not having money to study medicine, even after being the first ranker and securing a merit ranking in my common entrance test, to completing a General Management Program from IIM-Ahmedabad, from not having anyone to fall back upon, to being the person whom others depended on and fell back on, from being depressed and in mental trauma to being the person who lit up others' lives with knowledge, love, sharing and caring, basically from being a victim to a victor. I discovered my Mojo, my magical charm with these secrets and now I want to share them with all of you!

Before you begin, please treat this book as a guide. Keep a journal and complete the exercises as you read each chapter.

I am so excited to be sharing this with you and hope that this book helps you in your journey of personal development.

A candle that is lit should not just melt and die, but light up 100 other candles before doing so! - Rinnku. G

CHAPTER ONE

SELF IMAGE

"Knowing others is wisdom

Knowing Yourself is Enlightenment"

-Lao Tzu"

Imagine this scene. Your company is hosting a grand function on its 10th anniversary. All employees have been invited and you are standing in front of a grand five star hotel. The *durban* smiles and opens the door for you and welcomes you in. As you walk in, you are awed by the huge, shining chandeliers, tall pillars of white and gold, hotel staff walking around in impeccable uniforms, the sweet scent rifting through the air, the lovely and well kept indoor plants in brass pots. You enter the banquet hall and see all your senior management and the founders of the company there.

What would you do now? Would you walk up to them and talk to them? Would you congratulate them on the company's 10th anniversary? Or would you quietly move to a corner with your drink, look around to find some familiar faces and talk to them.

What you would do, depends on your **Self-Image.**

Self Image is what you think of yourself, what you believe about yourself and what you feel about yourself.

If you feel good about yourself physically and mentally, you would not hesitate to talk to anyone, or to be yourself or to express yourself freely. However, if you feel little or wanting, if you feel not capable, not good enough, you would be having a low self image.

What you think about yourself, is what will manifest outside.

When you look into the mirror everyday, who do you see? Someone strong, someone beautiful, someone capable, someone loving, someone grateful for all the blessings, someone successful or the opposite of this?

Is it your fault that you are not self-confident, that you have a low self esteem? The answer is a **YES.**

But you may say, surely there are a lot of other factors that determine self confidence. Some of them being genetics, your background, where you come from? A small town or city, from a family where nobody speaks English, having parents who were poor, your nationality, your race, creed, your color etc. You may think that these factors have some role to play in it, and have some reason for you to feel low. The answer is *maybe*, but there is nothing that you cannot change, if you wish to be different. It may be difficult but not impossible.

History has so many examples of successful people who were once failures.

Mohandas Karamchand Gandhi, the man who is today called **'Mahatma'** by the world is the biggest example of what a positive Self Image can do. A barrister by profession, born to a rich family, he had everything one could ask for in terms of worldly success and material wealth. However, he chose to give it all up to fight for the right of freedom for Indians, the right of all human beings to be treated equally, to eradicate untouchability, to obtain equal rights for all human beings irrespective of race or color. He failed multiple times and his methods were questioned. He was jailed multiple times, however he stood strong. He believed in himself. He knew who he was, what he was doing and what he was capable of. His positive Self Image helped him attract millions of followers. His war weapons were 'Satya' and 'Ahimsa' (Truth and Non-Violence). The whole world thought how could a puny man who believed in fasting, non violently solve huge problems of colonialism and of foreign rule ? But Gandhiji had an awesome Self Image. He knew who he was and what his strengths were. He was confident that this was the only way we could have freedom. His strength lay in his obstinacy of purpose, his determination to never give up, his tolerance, his way of 'Satyagraha'. His ways ultimately helped India win Independence!

Amitabh Bachchan, the man whom we call 'Sadi ka Mahanayak' today was rejected by All India Radio. They said he could never be an artist on radio with that voice. But it is that very deep, resonating voice that has made him stand out today. He joined the movies and became famous as the 'Angry Young Man' of Indian Cinema. He went on to win awards for his performance. He was the ruling Superstar of his times. In one of his films, there was a fight scene and he got badly injured in it. In 1982, Amitabh Bachchan suffered a severe injury while shooting an action sequence with Puneet Issar in Bengaluru for Coolie. His co-star accidently hit him in the stomach which made Amitabh bleed profusely and he became unconscious. He was rushed to St. Philomena's hospital for an emergency operation. Post this, he was shifted to Mumbai's Breach Candy hospital. He was declared 'clinically dead'. The whole nation was crying and praying for their Superstar.It was the nation's prayers that brought him back to life. He starred in many movies as the leading man. After years of tasting success at the box office, destiny stopped smiling on him. He failed miserably after starting his own production house. He was heavily in debt and would have been on the streets. But he did not give up. He sat down to reflect and think of solutions to his problems. He asked himself what he does best and said that it was acting. He knew how to act. So, he walked up to his friend, neighbor and well known director Yash Chopra's house. He implored him for work and' Mohabbatein' happened. But it was not just this movie that saved him. At a time when movie stars shunned TV, Amitabh Bachchan came on TV with the show 'Kaun Banega Crorepati'. He started doing ads for products like Chawanprash, hair oil, soft drinks etc to clear off his debt. People mocked him for what he was doing. But he continued working hard. Today, he is back on the big screen playing versatile roles. Roles that are now written for the older Amitabh, roles with substance, not just dancing around the trees or beating the villains black and blue. And today, he has recovered his lost glory, his lost wealth, all of it and how! His comeback is one of the most inspiring stories because there has been no star who has survived in Bollywood for 60 plus years. His story is one that has turbulence, multiple obstacles, never a smooth road, but he has been coming back strong every time. Rising every time he falls. And staying strong till date. An octogenarian, still working, coming on set for 'Kaun Banega Crorepati' and still acting in movies. His energy and enthusiasm for life are awesome. He has been battling so many health issues like diverticulitis of the small intestine and a rare autoimmune disease called myasthenia gravis. In spite of these health issues, he keeps himself busy working, socially engaged and active.

How do you think this was possible if not for his positive Self Image? Imagine what he would have been saying to himself every morning when he woke up and saw himself in the mirror? That brings us to another very important topic Self Talk or your Inner Dialogue.

Self Talk, Your Inner Dialogue is the reason behind your Self Confidence and Self Image. If you wake up in the morning and say Oh, one more day and the same old dreary work, so be it. That's how your day will be. But if you wake up with an attitude of gratitude and give thanks for just being alive, feeling hopeful and having enthusiasm, you will indeed have a joyful day. More on Self Talk in the later chapters.

Amitabh Bachchan believed in himself. He recognized his strengths and went on to work on them. He did not hesitate to ask for help when required. He remained humble and had the dignity of labor. He had a positive Self-Image.

What is your Self Image?

Do you think you are a kitten or a lion? Take the Rosenberg test below and find out.

	STATEMENT	Strongly Agree	Agree	Disagree	Strongly Disagree
1	I feel that I am a person of worth, at least on an equal plane with others.				
2	I feel that I have a number of good qualities.				
3	All in all, I am inclined to feel that I am a failure.				
4	I am able to do things as well as most other people.				
5	I feel I do not have much to be proud of.				
6	I take a positive attitude toward myself.				
7	On the whole, I am satisfied with myself.				
8	I wish I could have more respect for myself.				
9	I certainly feel useless at times.				
10	At times I think I am no good at all.				

Scoring: Max-30 points

For questions 1,2,4,6,7

A. Strongly Agree-3 points
B. Agree- 2 points
C. Disagree-1 point
D. Strongly Disagree- 0 points

For questions 3,5,8,9

A. Strongly Agree-0 points
B. Agree- 1 points
C. Disagree-2 point
D. Strongly Disagree- 3 points

If you have a score of less than 15 it means you have low self -esteem.

To understand oneself is the most important discovery that one can do. One who knows herself has conquered everything. Is knowing oneself easy? How do we become what we have become? Can we change ourselves if we wish to do so? This is where the magic of the human mind comes into picture, which we shall explore in the next chapter.

Summary:

1. Life is a series of ups and downs. Turbulence in life is a given
2. The person who is successful is the one who knows how to ride through the turbulence of life without giving up
3. To know oneself is the most important discovery.
4. Self Image is what you think, believe and feel about yourself
5. You can change yourself and your circumstances if you work on your Self Image
6. A positive self image is a result of positive Self Talk and mastering your mind

CHAPTER TWO

MAGICAL MIND

"Rule your mind or it will rule you"

-Unknown

The human mind is marvelous, and we are at its command every second mechanically doing tasks, responding without paying any thought to it. The mind is your master, and you are its slave. So many people go about life doing the same things that they do, expecting different results. It is said that old habits die hard and they are difficult to change.

Let us understand how the human mind works.

According to Sigmund Freud, the mind consists of three parts, the Conscious mind, the SubConscious and the Unconscious. The Conscious mind is the one with which we can sense an external stimulus and trigger a reaction to it. Based on the event and the situation, it then stores that reaction either in the Subconscious or the Unconscious Mind.

The Subconscious mind is the one where past memory is stored and can be accessed whenever required, pretty much like the RAM of a computer. It is there to use when required. It contains your CURRENT thoughts and feelings.

Have you experienced recalling the lyrics of your favorite song when the song is playing on the radio but not remembering it otherwise. You somehow just know the lyrics when the song is on and hum along. This is because the Subconscious mind has stored it and helped you recall it when you wanted it.

The Unconscious mind is the place where your deepest desires, thoughts, feelings, emotions which are usually repressed through trauma or have been programmed while growing up reside. This is the place from which your behavioral patterns and habits have formed. Years of programming due to external conditioning, taking in suggestions from the external world has made you behave the way you do. If in trauma or in a comfort zone, this is the behavior that you would naturally revert to.

Please read out this word aloud SILK.

Now answer this question. What do cows drink?

.

.

...

.....

....

....

Did you answer Milk?

Now think about this one more time. What do cows drink?

Not milk for sure. Cows GIVE and not DRINK milk.

Ha! Ha! Ha! Tricked you, didn't it?

Why do you think this happened?

Because you have stored memories and associations in your mind about Cow and Milk. And Milk rhymes with Silk. So, your mind put two and two together and picked up the answer that was the easiest association, the one that made you expend the least energy, not necessarily the most accurate answer! Our mind is very lazy and is meant to protect us and help us survive. It does not like to expend a lot of energy. It is meant to be energy efficient. Thinking, analyzing, making decisions, all take up a lot of energy. So, what it does is, pick up the stored answer and reproduce it.

Have you noticed that you usually have a pattern in which you do your daily chores? You sleep on the same side of the bed, wake up at almost the same time every day, you get ready and drive to work almost mechanically without even needing to check a map because the map is stored in your mind. This is because you have got used to doing things the same way. The mind likes to keep things predictable and energy efficient! Changes are disliked and take time to become behavior and habits.

So, how is our behavior formed?

Our behavior is a result of multiple factors. Over the years many behavioral scientists and psychologists have come up with various theories on how behavior is formed.

Nature Vs Nurture: Kurt Lewin was one of the first psychologists to propose that the development of an individual was the product of the interaction between inborn predispositions (nature) and life experiences (nurture).

The behavior of the individual is formed by ***Nature* of the** individual due to the internal environment like genetics, thoughts or intentions, beliefs and ***Nurture*** due to external environment like motivations, external triggers or influences like school, friends, books that one reads, culture, nationality etc.

This concept was presented by Lewin in the form of a mathematical equation known as Lewin's Equation for behavior, stating that behavior is the function of the person interacting within his environment or $B = f\ (P,E)$.

This means that every individual has different internal and external triggers that shape their behavior. This explains why two children born in the same house will still have different behavior because each one's nature and nurture would have been different.

Also, since the behavior of an individual changes based on the environment it is not enough just to know the nature of the person, it is important to observe the effects of the environment on the person too.

Nature of the individual

It is said that a baby's brain starts developing very early. In just the fifth week after conception, the first synapses begin forming in a fetus's spinal cord. Just about the end of the second trimester, the cerebral cortex, which is responsible for most of what we think of as mental life–conscious experience, voluntary actions, thinking, remembering, and feeling starts beginning to function. In the last trimester, fetuses are capable of simple forms of learning, like habituating (decreasing their startle response) to a repeated auditory stimulus, such as a loud clap just outside the mother's abdomen. Several studies have shown that newborn babies respond to familiar odors (such as their own amniotic fluid) and sounds (such as a maternal heartbeat or their own mother's voice). Despite these rather sophisticated abilities, babies enter the world with a still-primitive cerebral cortex, and it is the gradual maturation of this complex part of the brain that explains much of their emotional and cognitive maturation in the first few years of life. Babies do carry some of the 'memories and knowledge' of what they hear inside the mother's womb. It is stored away in the Subconscious mind to be brought into play into life when required.

The great Indian saint Vyasa wrote about the play of nature centuries ago in the great epic 'Mahabharata'. The Mahabharata is the story of the Pandavas and the Kauravas.

Abhimanyu was the son of Arjuna, one of the five Pandavas. It is said that Abhimanyu learnt the art of penetrating the 'Chakravyuha' (a war formation) while he was in his mother Subhadra's womb. Arjuna was narrating how the Chakravyuha was formed to her when she was pregnant with Abhimanyu. However, Subhadra fell asleep halfway and only heard how one could penetrate the Chakravyuha and did not hear how one could get out. Abhimanyu used this knowledge in the battle of Kurukshetra against the Kauravas. He got into the chakravyuha and fought bravely but was ultimately killed as he did not know how to come out of it.

Nurture of the individual

Life experiences are of paramount importance in shaping the behavior of the individual. The country that you are born in, your parents, teachers, religion, beliefs are all external influences which shape you into the human being that you are.

Nurture assumes that correlations between environmental factors and psychological outcomes are caused environmentally. For example, how much parents read with their children and how well children learn to read appear to be related. Other examples include environmental stress and its effect on depression. It is said that 'tell me who your friends are and I shall tell you who you are" Our environment does have an effect on who we become and how we behave.

So, what is important: Nature or Nurture?

Instead of defending extreme nativist or nurturist views, most psychological researchers are now interested in investigating how nature and nurture interact.

For example, Epigenetics states that environmental influences affect the expression of genes. Epigenetics is an emerging area of scientific research that shows how environmental influences-children's experiences actually affect the expression of their genes.

This means that the old debate that the genes are 'set in stone' has been disproven. Nature vs Nurture is no longer a debate. It's nearly always both! We now talk about the neuroplasticity of the brain and the ability to form new habits and behaviors. This is possible by making the unconscious conscious. Which means that we need to become aware of all that we do on autopilot, our thoughts, our beliefs, our attitudes are all shaping who we become. And the first step to changing behavior is ***Self-awareness.***

Summary:

1. The mind is magical consisting of the Conscious, the Unconscious and the Subconscious.

2. The Conscious mind responds to external stimuli and triggers.

3. The Subconscious mind stores past memories and helps retrieve it whenever you want. It houses your current feelings and emotions as you retrieve those memories.

4. The Unconscious mind houses your deepest fears, thoughts, emotions that are repressed through trauma or programmed as you grew up.

5. Our behavior is shaped by Nature and Nurture both.

6. Our environment has a huge effect on who we become.

7. It is possible to change our behavior by becoming self-aware of who we are.

CHAPTER THREE

ATTITUDES

"Our attitude in life determines life's attitude towards us" -John Mitchell

An attitude refers to a set of emotions, beliefs, and behaviours toward a particular object, person, thing, or event. Attitudes are often the result of experience or upbringing, and they can have a powerful influence over behaviour. While attitudes are enduring, they can also change.

What's your opinion on women driving cars in Saudi Arabia? What do you think about global warming? Should children have access to the internet? What do you think about wearing a mask or lock-downs during this pandemic?

Chances are that you have fairly strong opinions on the above subjects. You have developed attitudes on these subjects which influence your beliefs and your behaviour.

So, how are attitudes formed?

Attitudes as a learned tendency to evaluate things in a certain way. This can include evaluations of people, issues, objects, or events. Such evaluations are often positive or negative, but they can also be uncertain at times.

For example, you might have mixed feelings about a particular person or issue. Researchers also suggest that there are several different components that make up attitudes. The components of attitudes are sometimes referred to as CAB or the ABC's of attitude.

Components of Attitude

- **Cognitive Component:** Your thoughts and beliefs about the subject
- **Affective Component:** How the object, person, issue, or event makes you feel
- **Behavioral Component:** How attitude influences your behaviour

Attitudes can also be explicit and implicit. Explicit attitudes are those that we are consciously aware of and that clearly influence our behaviours and beliefs. Implicit attitudes are unconscious but still have an effect on our beliefs and behaviours.

Attitudes are formed due to a number of factors like Experience, Social Factors, Learning, Conditioning and Observation.

A child who touches a hot rod learns from experience that touching something hot will scald the skin. Society has its own norms and rules of behaviour. There are things that are considered appropriate. For example: spitting on the road is considered inappropriate.

Learning through classical conditioning shapes attitudes. In a television commercial, you see a young man taking huge risks, jumping from trucks, or crossing a huge chasm in one leap and then pulling out a bottle of the cold drink and sipping it victoriously. This causes you to develop a positive association with this particular beverage and makes you believe that this drink is for those who are or want to be portrayed as brave and adventurous.

Finally, people also learn attitudes by observing people around them. When someone you admire greatly espouses a particular attitude, you are more likely to develop the same beliefs. For example, children spend a great deal of time observing the attitudes of their parents and usually begin to demonstrate similar outlooks. Also, this is where the influence of role models matter. Who you choose as a role model has a lot to do with what and who you become.

Our thoughts trigger emotions in us and over a period of time it becomes our belief. For example: If as a child, you saw a snake come into your garden and your mother screamed and moved you away from it hastily, you associate the emotion of fear with a snake. So, every time you see a snake, you experience the same emotion of fear. Your body might start showing the same reactions of fear, teeth chattering, shivering etc. And you start believing that snakes are poisonous and dangerous.

Now, it is a known fact that are harmless snakes too. If you were the child of a snake-catcher, your emotional response and consequent behaviour would have been totally different. You might probably pick up a stick and lift the snake and put it into a basket fearlessly. So, our thoughts trigger emotions which trigger actions (behaviour)

Your attitude depends on the thoughts you put in or others have put in to your head while you were growing up.

Summary:

1. Attitude is a set of emotions, beliefs and behaviour towards a person, thing, situation
2. Attitudes are learned tendencies
3. Attitudes are formed through conditioning
4. Your thoughts become emotions which then become actions or behaviour

CHAPTER FOUR

YOUR BELIEF SYSTEM

"Man is what he believes"

-Anton Chekov

Beliefs are what shapes a human being. Beliefs either make or break us. As we grow up, we interact with a lot of people, we observe a lot of things happening around us. Some of it we perceive as pleasant and some unpleasant. We keep storing away this information in our subconscious mind for years. Like we saw in chapter 2, on a day to day basis, we operate on auto mode based on the beliefs that we have stored in our mind.

If your parents were proud of you as a child, you grow up to be confident and willing to tackle all challenges.

If your teacher said to you, that learning a language was not easy for you because you came from another region, then you probably struggled to learn that language.

If your friends said you had a good sense of humor and loved being around you, you might find it easy to socialize.

Beliefs can be empowering or limiting.

An empowering belief is one that makes you happy, inspires you and helps you grow as a person.

A limiting belief instils fear in you, makes you worry, keeps you anxious and keeps you unhappy and stunted in your growth.

Beliefs can be called faith, religion, superstition, tradition, culture and so many other things. If you look at the root of all these things, it is nothing but belief. It is said that 'Faith moves mountains', and this is true. You become what you believe in.

Gandhiji said "Sow a thought, reap an action.

Sow an action, reap a habit.

Sow a habit, reap your character.

Sow your character and you reap your destiny."

Beliefs begin with a small thought in your head. A thought that evokes emotion becomes a belief. Much has been said about the power of thought. Napolean Hill said' Think and Grow Rich' and has written a whole book on this subject.

What you believe in makes or breaks you. It is important for you to have empowering thoughts as these will become your beliefs, habits that get stored in our subconscious mind, it will become the way you respond to external stimuli. Whether you sit down and start crying, became frustrated, angry, weak and give up OR rise up to the challenge life throws at you, depends on what you believe in.

Let us look at some examples of people who lived with empowering beliefs and rose above all kinds of adversity.

Sudha Chandran (born 27 September 1965) is an Indian film and television actress and an accomplished Bharatanatyam dancer. In May 1981, at about 16 years old, in Tamil Nadu, Chandran met with an accident in which her legs were wounded. She received initial medical treatment of her injuries at a local hospital and was later admitted to Vijaya Hospital at Madras. After doctors discovered that gangrene had formed on her right leg, amputation was required. Sudha says that this period was the toughest time of her life. She subsequently regained some mobility with the help of a prosthetic Jaipur foot.She returned to dancing after a gap of two years and performed in India, Saudi Arabia, United States, UK, Canada, UAE, Qatar, Kuwait, Bahrain , Yemen and Oman . Her biography is part of the curriculum for school children in the age group of 8-11 years. Sudha Chandran started her career with a Telugu film Mayuri, which was based on her own life. The film was later dubbed in Tamil and Malayalam.It was also remade in Hindi as 'Naache Maayuri', where Sudha again played herself and co-starred with Shekhar Suman, Aruna Irani and Dina Pathak. She was awarded the 1986 Special Jury Award at the National Film Awards for her performance in Mayuri.

Another example is ***Arunima Sinha***. A former national volleyball and football player, Arunima was thrown out of a moving train by a couple of perverts who tried to rob her but eventually failed. She fell on a parallel track and was immediately run over by a passing train and lost her leg. But her disability didn't restrain her to achieve a feat that only a few have achieved thus far, in the whole wide world. She reached the summit of Mount Everest at 10:55 AM on 21 May 2013 and became the only one in doing so.

Arunachalam Muruganathan, the man who gave India's rural women affordable sanitary pads. There are men who squirm at the mention of a woman's period. Then there's Muruganantham, a school drop-out, who **re-engineered a sanitary machine which makes about 120 napkins an hour**. Currently more than 1300 machines made by his start-up company are installed across 27 states in India and seven other countries. Receiving the award from the Indian president was not the happiest moment of his life. But his proudest moment came after he installed a machine in a remote village in Uttarakhand, in the foothills of the Himalayas.

Sanjit 'Bunker' Roy runs the 'Barefoot College' The college gives simple school lessons in reading, writing and accounting to adults and children. It works to impart skills people's need in their everyday lives. The most sought after students are "drop-outs, cop-outs and wash-outs". He has helped over **1000 villages in 37 countries**

to get electrification with solar power. The 'Barefoot approach' may be viewed as a 'concept', 'solution', 'revolution', 'design' or an 'inspiration' but it is really a simple message that can easily be replicated by the poor and for the poor in neglected and underprivileged communities anywhere the world.

Jockin Arputham, the 'Toilet Man' Arputham was born in Kolar Gold Fields, near Bangalore, in the south of India. He moved to Mumbai when he was 18 to work as a carpenter. Having no place to live in, he began sleeping outside people's houses in Janata Colony, a slum of around 70,000 people. When the inhabitants of the slum were threatened with eviction, he united the community in organizing protests and fighting injustice. **Over the years, Arputham has built 30,000 houses in India, and 1,00,000 houses abroad.** For his remarkable work, he has been awarded the Padma Shri. He didn't win the Nobel Peace Prize but Jockin Sir has dedicated his life to bring peace for slum dwellers.

These are not all. India has so many examples of people who overcame their adversities with their empowering beliefs!

Exercise: Time to work on a Belief Diagnosis now.

Choose a quiet place to sit down. Take a journal and a pen. Start thinking about all the beliefs that you had as a child with respect to the following:

a. Yourself as a person- physically, mentally, emotionally- Are you patient, strong willed, quick to cry etc?

a. Your relationships-family, friends, neighbors, spouse, partner- how do you describe these relationships?

c. Money and your relationship with it- Do you believe that money does not grow on trees, the rich are corrupt, it takes a lot of hard work to become rich, you never have enough, or do you believe that money is something that comes to you easily.

d. Your work, colleagues, boss- What do you believe about them? They are helpful, supportive, or trying to pull you down all the time.

e. Your attitude- Positive, enabling, defeatist , pessimistic?

f. Your spirituality- Do you believe that the universe works to help you get what you want, God is always there to take your burdens and show you the way?

g. Your culture, traditions, superstitions- What are the beliefs that have been passed down to you? You started believing some things after something you experienced?

Write with present tense and start each sentence with

- Something that I believe about myself is________________
- Something that I believe about relationships is____________

- Something that I believe about money is________________
- Something that I believe about spirituality is______________

Don't judge your thoughts, don't say "Oh I am not like this now", don't justify anything. Just write it down.

Some of you may find this exercise easy to do with many things coming up as you write. some of you may take longer and might need more time.

Whatever it is, take time, spend time with yourself in silence and journal everything that you believe in. Do it no matter what, even if it takes multiple sessions of self-reflection time.

Summary:

1. A thought that evokes emotion becomes a belief.
2. Beliefs can be empowering or limiting.
3. Empowering beliefs help you grow as a person and achieve happiness, success, and abundance in all areas of your life.
4. Limiting beliefs are making you die day by day and stopping you from growing.
5. You are a result of all your beliefs.

CHAPTER FIVE

OVERCOMING LIMITATIONS

"All personal breakthroughs begin with a change in beliefs. So how do we change? The most effective way is to get your brain to associate massive pain to the old belief. You must feel deep in your gut that not only has this belief cost you pain in the past, but it's costing you in the present and, ultimately,
can only bring you pain in the future. Then you must associate tremendous pleasure to the idea of adopting a new, empowering belief."

- Anthony Robbins

One day a man met Ratan Tata in a plane. He walked up to him and told him how much he admires him and his work. Then he asked him if he could get his autograph and Ratan Tata said yes. The man was overjoyed and started looking for a pen in his pocket and in his bag. Unable to find a pen, he looked sheepishly at Ratan Tata and said no matter what he did, he seemed to keep losing pens. Ratan Tata smiled, took out his own pen and gave him an autograph. The man asked him how he could stop losing pens. To which, Ratan Tata told him to buy the most expensive pen there ever is.

After a couple of years, the man was in the same plane with Ratan Tata again, who recognised him and asked him if he had stopped losing pens by now. The man beamed and showed him a pen with a gold nib. The man then thanked Ratan Tata for the wonderful tip and said that he was surprised that he was no longer losing pens now. To this Ratan Tata said that the limitation was not the habit of losing pens, but in his mind, and the value that he attached to the pen. Now that the pen had a gold nib, the man valued it more and hence was always careful of picking it up and putting it back in his pocket every time he finished using it to write. And hence he never lost his pen again.

The story above is a simple illustration of how limitations in our mind takes over our behavior and personalities.

It is only when we feel a deep pain about losing something or attach great value to something that we change our habits. We either do things because it causes us deep pain or great pleasure.

Exercise time again. What are your biggest fears?

Take out your journal and start answering these questions.

1. Do you fear being successful? What if you get so successful that you lose everyone you love in your life? What if you are lonely at the top?
2. Do you fear failure? What if you fail? How will you face the world? Will it be too embarrassing? Will you be ashamed of yourself?
3. Do you fear that you are not skilled/not an expert/ not good enough to achieve your goal?
4. Do you fear being unloved or not being able to love anyone?
5. Do you fear rejection which in turn makes you lose self-esteem and self-confidence? Do you avoid meeting people?
6. Do you fear stereotypes- Being of a certain race, color, financial standards, nationality, gender, etc

Now that you have written your answers down, close the book. Let it stay for a night. Open it the next day or after a few days and read your answers.

Now, think about your answers. Do you find factual evidence to substantiate your fears?

Do you realize that all these fears only exist in your head?

None of them are real.

Mahatma Gandhi said "Nobody can make you feel inferior other than yourself"

These beliefs only limit your growth and success. They stop you from achieving your peak potential, from being the best version of yourself. They keep you small, afraid and meek. They prevent you from discovering your true hidden talent.

So, how do you overcome these limiting beliefs? Here are 3 tips to overcome them.

TIP No 1: YET

You change these limiting beliefs by changing the words that you say to yourself. Words are powerful. They can make or break you.

If you have this limiting belief that you can't do something, for example, if you are saying to yourself that "I can't sing very well" Replace this sentence with " I can't sing very well YET"

I can't seem to memorize things YET. I can't code as well YET. I can't cook as well YET.

You see what adding the word YET does. It gives you hope. It changes the whole narrative in your head. It changes the outlook. Yes, you can't do something now, but surely you are going to learn to do it better.

TIP No 2: IMAGINE

Every time you fear failure or losing people that you love, or feel you are not good enough, just imagine the complete opposite of the situation. For example: If you fear that your presentation in front of your boss is going to be bad, just IMAGINE that the boss is so pleased with you and actually applauds you.

If you fear walking up to your parents and telling them that you love someone, IMAGINE that they are happily accepting your partner and having a cup of tea with him/ her.

You have an examination to pass, and you have studied hard for it but still have the fear of the examination. Imagine that you are seeing your name on the results board, right on top of the list.

The power of imagination is profound. It is important to really IMAGINE the details of the situation that you want to create for yourself. What is your boss saying to you? What are your parents saying? Where are you sitting and having tea? What will you say exactly? What are your friends and teachers telling you after seeing your results? How are you feeling? Get down to the details and IMAGINE the situation you want to create. Create the vision in your mind first. You can also create a vision board of pictures that represent the life you want to create. You can doodle in your journal.

Everything begins with your thoughts and imagination. The seed of imagination can bring forth manifestation. You will be amazed at the results it will create in your life.

TIP No 3: A Magic Mantra

One more way of overcoming limitations is to have a magic mantra. This does not have to be religious. It is a mantra that you create for yourself. Any sentence that is uplifting for you, that rejuvenates you, that reminds you of your greatness and inspires you.

Every time I am down and out, my mantra is *'This too shall pass'*

Some other mantras that work for me are chanting the name of my guru when I feel lost and am looking for direction.

When I am feeling that I lack the skill or experience to do something, I look at myself in the mirror and say " *I am a rockstar. I can do this*"

When I am thinking of something negative, I say " CANCEL, CANCEL" and imagine erasing those words off my mind.

What is your magic mantra? Think about it and write it down. You can do it!

Exercise: Write down in your journal which of the three tips would you use?

After you try using these tips, write down what impact it has on you and in your life in your daily journal.

Summary:

- Examine your deepest fears. Recognize them and write them down.
- Use the 3 tips to overcome your fears- the word 'Yet', the power of 'Imagination' and your own unique magic mantra.
- Say: I cannot swim yet. The word 'yet' added to the end of the sentence replaces the fear of being unskilled to swim with a hope that you can do it in future.
- The power of imagination helps you create the picture of success in your mind first before it becomes a reality. Every successful invention, discovery, famous personality first had to create a picture of the success in their mind.
- Making a vision board and pasting pictures of what you want to achieve helps you in realizing your dreams.
- We can overcome our limiting beliefs by changing our vocabulary and adopting unique magic mantras.

CHAPTER SIX

YOUR INNER DIALOGUE

"The capacity for inner dialogue is the touchstone of outer objectivity"

-Carl Jung

If you are a fan of Indian movies, you would have definitely watched scenes in which the protagonist is caught in a dilemma and their alter self comes out and talks to them. They are usually clad in different clothes from the protagonist. If they are giving good advice, then they are shown clad in white. They are talking them out of the bad things they are about to do. Sometimes, the alter self is bad and is shown clad in black and giving wrong advice and egging them on to do the incorrect, unethical thing.

Just like they show in the movies, our inner voice is speaking to us all the time. It keeps telling us 1000 different things. It propels us to act, sometimes good and sometimes not so good.

The year 2020 was the year the world witnessed the 'Covid Pandemic'. A crisis that no one thought would occur. The impact it had on people's lives, economies of the world was devastating. Social distancing became the norm. People were wearing masks. Oxygen, something that we never paid attention to, was becoming scarce.

This was the time when companies had to get innovative. Work from home options were given to those who could do this. Now, was the Covid Pandemic a blessing or a curse?

As you battled the pandemic and worked from home, studied online and stayed indoors all the time, did you lose the enthusiasm to get up and get dressed? Were you lounging around in your pajamas, waking up late and just putting off a lot of work, thinking that you can get it done later? The inner voice must be saying" Sleep a little more, the meeting is at 10 AM only" or "Just watch one more episode on Netflix"

OR

Did your inner voice say" Wow, now that you have a lot of time, learn to play the guitar, or bake, or try Yoga"

Whatever you chose to do, that choice would have empowered your life or completely destroyed it.

I know of people who have completed multiple certifications, learnt new skills like embroidery, cooking, gardening, started home based businesses or pursued their hobbies like painting, music, mandala art etc and become a happier, better version of themselves. And

I know of people who just kept binge eating, binge watching TV, put on a tremendous amount of weight and developed health issues because of it.

Our inner voice is there to help us survive. It wants to keep us protected from unpredictable changes. So, you will have to have a dialogue with your Inner Voice every time it talks to you. Don't let it be a monologue. Don't let it instruct you every time. And don't try to shoo it away. Every time you try to chase it away, it will keep coming back to hound you. In the last chapter, we learnt about beliefs. You might be trying to break some of your limiting beliefs.

Let's take the belief of not feeling good enough. It happens to the best of us. The best speakers, coaches, leaders, actors, authors all go through this feeling. There is always a little bit of nervousness and butterflies every time they walk up on stage or there is a new book released or they must launch a new project etc. Their Inner Voice might be stopping them and saying" This is not good enough, it is not perfect, people will ridicule you, you are going to make a fool of yourself" etc. Now, they have 2 choices, one to listen to the Inner Voice and get affected by it and step back, or two to listen to the Inner voice and move on anyway.

Tips to Master the Inner Voice

1. Listen and Thank -Always listen to the inner voice and say, '*Thank you for sharing*'! It is only trying to protect you. Do not fret if it is a negative thought. Say '*Thank you for sharing'!*

2. Give your Inner Voice a Name - Is there someone whom you don't like? Someone who keeps ranting in your home? A character in the movies or books you read. Just give your Inner Voice their name and every time it says something negative, say " there goes Chacha again" or 'Ranting Ruby' or 'Pappu paglait' or whatever you want to call it. Eases the situation with a bit of humor, doesn't it? :-)

3. Have a dialogue - Talk back to it. Act like your inner voice is a person. Ask what is really worrying you? Say that you have got things covered and go through the checklist in your head. For example: If you need to be on stage to speak or make a presentation in a meeting, and your inner voice is dissuading you from doing it, talk to it, say thank you for sharing. I have my presentation all formatted well, have got the bullet points written down in a piece of paper, have checked it for spelling errors and worse case if something still goes wrong like a technical glitch, I shall smile and breathe in and breathe out till it comes back on!

4. Carry your genie - Have a physical object with you that will remind you to not think negative or to stop the negative Inner Voice. You can wear a wristband that reads- You are marvelous! You are the best! You can do it! Or any other uplifting message on it. Snap it on your wrist to remind you to think positive. You can carry a rock in your pocket and touch it every time you feel anxious. You could carry a picture of your deity or wear a finger ring with your deity or a special gemstone on it if that makes you feel good. These objects act like Aladdin's magical lamp. Rub your magical object, your genie when anxious. Imagine the genie coming out and saying "Your wish is my command! Whatever the genie is, touch it when you feel anxious.

Exercise: Which of the above will you use? Take some time to write it down.

Summary:

- Your Inner Voice is there to protect you.
- Always listen to it and do not shoo it away.
- Say Thank you for sharing every time your inner voice talks to you.
- Give your Inner Voice a name. Give it a persona.
- Learn to have a dialogue with your inner voice.
- Carry your magical genie with you all the time and touch it when anxious.
- Mastering your Inner Voice will go a long way in helping you reach your goals, whatever they may be.

CHAPTER SEVEN

YOUR BEHAVIOR

"Knowing your own darkness is the best method for dealing with the darknesses of other people."

-Carl Jung

We learnt in Chapter 3 that Attitudes are thoughts, emotions and behavior all put together. From time immemorial, people have been fascinated by human behavior. If we need to get somewhere in life, it is necessary to know why we behave the way we do. Why are we happy, motivated, energetic at times and sad, demotivated, completely feeling de-energised at times? Have you heard the Hindi saying " *Gali main sher aur ghar me bhigi billi'* (Lion outside and wet cat at home) meaning someone who behaves courageous and displays leadership outside just becomes a meek follower at home.

Have you noticed that some people are soft spoken, calm and quiet when they are in front of others, but the moment they get into their cars, they start driving like they own the road and you are wondering what happened to the quiet person, calm person?

Some persons may make grand plans and give great speeches but cannot sit down and execute their own plans.

Some people are the life of the party. Wherever they go, they are smiling, greeting people and seem to have a lot of friends around. Some people struggle to strike a conversation in a party while they have great conversations with the same person when it's one-on-one.

Why does this happen? We might be quick to judge these people as hypocrites or having two faces, but we all behave differently in different situations. We have various triggers, motivators and demotivators that make us behave differently. And as we learnt in Chapter 2, so much of our behavior is on auto-pilot. So, unless we learn to have conscious awareness of our behavior, we will not change it and will continue to behave the same way and produce the same results day after day.

Many behavioral scientists, psychologists, philosophers have been studying human behavior now for years. And the attempt is to understand it and master it so that we as human beings can master our lives.

Let us learn about the evolution of the study of human behavior and understand how behavior was interpreted over the ages.

The Four Roots Theory of Empedocles

One of the most interesting of these Pre-Socratic philosophers was Empedocles of Acragas(469 BC). As a philosopher, Empedocles is best known for his theory that the world is composed of four elements or, more precisely, 'roots' – fire, air, earth, and water.

In one of Empedocles' fragments, it is written thus: "Hear first the four roots of all things: shining Zeus (commonly identified as fire) and life-bringing Hera (commonly identified as air) and Aidoneus (commonly identified as earth) and Nestis (commonly identified as water)." This has become

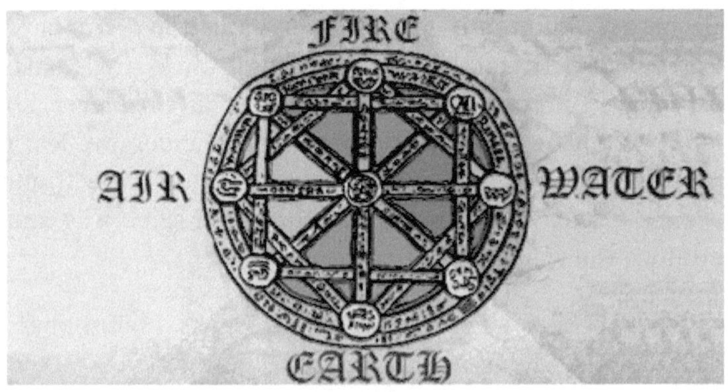

famous as the 'The Four Roots Theory of Empedocles' Empedocles devised the theory that all substances are made of four pure, indestructible elements: air, fire, water, and earth. This includes people who display the traits of Fire, Air, Water and Earth.

Hippocrates 4 temperaments or humors

Hippocrates in 370 BC theorized that personality traits and human behaviors are based on four separate temperaments associated with four fluids ("humors") of the body:

- Choleric temperament (yellow bile from the liver)
- Melancholic temperament (black bile from the kidneys)
- Sanguine temperament (red blood from the heart), and
- Phlegmatic temperament (white phlegm from the lungs)

Centuries later, the influential Greek physician and philosopher Galen built on Hippocrates's theory, suggesting that both diseases and personality differences could be explained by imbalances in the humors and that each person exhibits one of the four temperaments. For example, the choleric person is passionate, ambitious, and bold; the melancholic person is reserved, anxious, and unhappy; the sanguine person is joyful, eager, and optimistic; and the phlegmatic person is calm, reliable, and thoughtful

Galen's theory was prevalent for over 1,000 years and continued to be popular through the Middle Ages.

In the centuries after Galen, other researchers contributed to the development of his four primary temperament types, most prominently Immanuel Kant (in the 18th century) and psychologist Wilhelm Wundt (in the 19th century). Kant agreed with Galen that everyone could be sorted into one of the four temperaments and that there was no overlap between the four categories. He developed a list of traits that could be used to describe the personality of a person from each of the four temperaments. However, Wundt suggested that a better description of personality could be achieved using two major axes: emotional/nonemotional and changeable/ unchangeable. The first axis separated strong from weak emotions (the melancholic and choleric temperaments from the phlegmatic and sanguine). The second axis divided the changeable temperaments (choleric and sanguine) from the unchangeable ones (melancholic and phlegmatic)

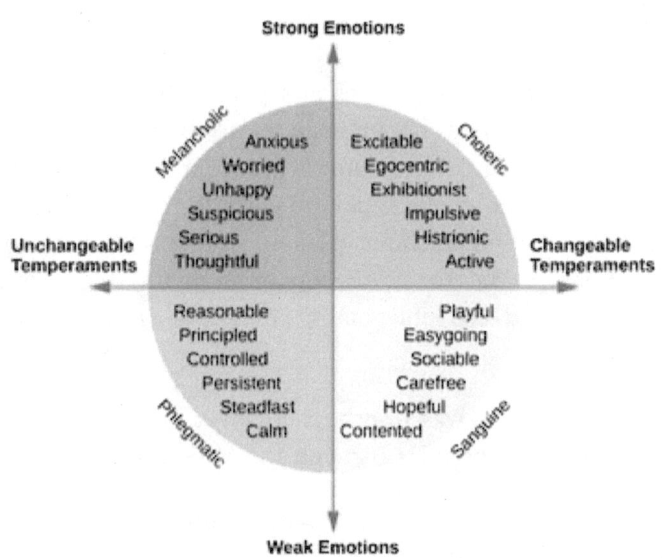

Zodiac Signs under Astrology

The Zodiac signs or ' Rashis' as we call them in Vedic Astrology also are classified into Air, Water, Earth and Fire signs. Based on which sign you belong to, you display the behavioral traits of the elements. There are 12 Zodiac Signs in all.

Fire Signs- Aries, Leo and Sagittarius

Earth Signs-Taurus, Virgo and Capricorn

Air Signs- Gemini, Libra and Aquarius

Water Signs-Cancer, Scorpio and Pisces

Fire Signs are described as spontaneous, reactive, courageous, passionate, creative, leaders, idealists, innovators, enthusiastic, assertive.

Earth Signs are described as reliable, dependable, practical, sensual, materialistic, cautious, realists, pragmatic

Air Signs are described as intellectual, detached, fair-minded, just, social, intuitive and humanitarian.

Water Signs are described as fluid, emotional, nurturing, pscyhic, deep, private, compassionate and impressionable

So, based on which Zodiac sign you belong to, you might be displaying the behavioral traits of the element that it is associated with.

Personality traits based on Ayurveda

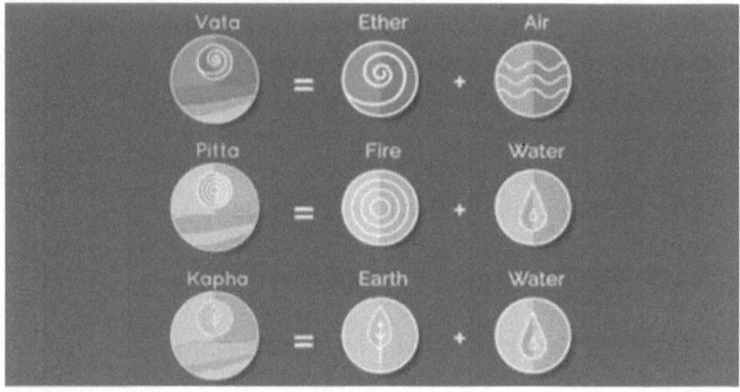

According to Ayurveda, the human body has three doshas(Tridosha) Vata, Pitta and Kapha. The 'Prakriti' or temperament of the person is determined by which of these dosha's are dominant. Ayurveda also defines 'Trigunas' Sattva, Rajas and Tamas. The temperament of the individual is based on the Tridosha and Triguna's The Prakriti of each individual is specific to that person. The behavior exhibited by individuals depending on the dominance of one or the other *Dosha* or *Guna* that is constitutionally present in the person from conception—is referred to as the particular *Prakriti–Guna* combination that a person exhibits.

Psychologically, the Vata dosha governs communication, creativity, flexibility, and quickness of thought. A balanced Vata individual is active, creative, and gifted with a natural gift of expressing themselves and communicating.

Pitta governs joy, intellect, courage, willpower, anger, jealousy, and mental perception. The balanced Pitta individual is blessed with a joyful disposition, a sharp intellect, and tremendous courage and drive.

Psychologically, Kapha governs love, patience, forgiveness, greed, attachment, and mental inertia. With the earthly element in its make up, Kapha grounds Vata and Pitta and helps offset imbalances related to these doshas.

The Gunas

Sattvic Guna - is the spiritual quality. Strength Respect for Gurus, nonviolence, meditation, kindness, silence, self-control, and purity of character are the motive force of sattvic action.There is a resolute constancy of mind and senses. When sattva is prevalent, the light of wisdom shines through the individual. Sattvic intellect clearly understands the difference between desirable and undesirable, undutiful and dutiful action

Rajasic Guna - Rajas guna is the “active quality”. Rajas guna is considered to give rise to passion and desire, it causes greed, activity, undertaking of works, restlessness, and desire. Rajas dominant person is full of attachment, full of longings for fruits of action. Due to dominance of self-interest, the intellect gives distorted picture of right and wrong. Renunciation and detachment are not fostered by Rajas dominant person. Enthusiasm, interest, and activity are some of the attributes of this guna.

Tamasic Guna - Tamas guna is the "material quality". Tamas arises from hopes and illusions. Tamas produces ambiguity, idleness, fantasy, and persistence.

Characteristics of Tamas guna dominant people are cautious, apprehensive, and revengeful. Tamasic guna also suggests disillusionment and cynicism.

When Tamasic guna is dominant, a person derives happiness which originates and ends in self-delusion and miscomprehension. The positive manifestation of Tamas guna is willingness to work very hard.

Myer's Briggs Indicator

According to Carl G. Jung's theory of psychological types [Jung, 1971], people can be characterized by their preference of general attitude:

1. Extraverted (E) vs. Introverted (I),

their preference of one of the two functions of perception:

2. Sensing (S) vs. Intuition (N),

and their preference of one of the two functions of judging:

3. Thinking (T) vs. Feeling (F)

The three areas of preference introduced by Jung are dichotomies (i.e. bipolar dimensions where each pole represents a different preference). Jung also proposed that in a person one of the four functions above is dominant – either a function of perception or a function of judging. Isabel Briggs Myers, a researcher and practitioner of Jung's theory, proposed to see the judging-perceiving relationship as a fourth dichotomy influencing personality type [Briggs Myers, 1980].

4. Judging (J) vs. Perceiving (P)

The first criterion, Extraversion – Introversion, signifies the source and direction of a person's energy expression. An extravert's source and direction of energy expression is mainly in the external world, while an introvert has a source of energy mainly in their own internal world.

The second criterion, Sensing – Intuition, represents the method by which someone perceives information. Sensing means that a person mainly believes information he or she receives directly from the external world. Intuition means that a person believes mainly information he or she receives from the internal or imaginative world.

The third criterion, Thinking – Feeling, represents how a person processes information. Thinking means that a person makes a decision mainly through logic. Feeling means that, as a rule, he or she makes a decision based on emotion, i.e. based on what they feel they should do.

The fourth criterion, Judging – Perceiving, reflects how a person implements the information he or she has processed. Judging means that a person organizes all of his life events and, as a rule, sticks to his plans. Perceiving means that he or she is inclined to improvise and explore alternative options.

All possible permutations of preferences in the 4 dichotomies above yield 16 different combinations, or personality types, representing which of the two poles in each of the four dichotomies dominates in a person, thus defining 16 different personality types. Each personality type can be assigned a 4 letter acronym of corresponding combination of preferences:

The 16 personality types

ESTJ ISTJ ENTJ INTJ ESTP ISTP ENTP INTP ESFJ ISFJ ENFJ INFJ ESFP ISFP ENFP INFP

The first letter in the personality type acronym corresponds to the first letter of the preference of general attitude - "E" for extraversion and "I" for introversion.

The second letter in the personality type acronym corresponds to the preference within the sensing-intuition dimension: "S" stands for sensing and "N" stands for intuition.

The third letter in the personality type acronym corresponds to preference within the thinking-feeling pair: "T" stands for thinking and "F" stands for feeling.

The fourth letter in the personality type acronym corresponds a person's preference within the judging-perceiving pair: "J" for judging and "P" for perception.For example:

ISTJ stands for Introverted, Sensing, Thinking, Judging

ENFP stands for Extraverted, iNtuitive, Feeling, Perceiving

ISTJ Responsible, sincere, analytical, reserved, organized, trustworthy with sound practical judgment	**ISFJ** Warm, considerate, detailed, traditional, devoted caretakers who enjoy being helpful to others	**INFJ** Idealistic, organized, committed, creative, enjoy intellectual stimulation	**INTJ** Independent, visionary, strategic, reserved, driven by their own original ideas to achieve improvements
ISTP Self-determined, action-oriented, adventurous, logical, skilled at understanding how mechanical things work	**ISFP** Caring, adaptable, realistic, flexible, seek to create a personal environment that is practical and beautiful	**INFP** Compassionate, empathetic, loyal, caring, focus on dreams and possibilities	**INTP** Theoretical, reserved, intellectual, imaginative, original thinkers who enjoy speculations
ESTP Pragmatic, versatile, out-going action-oriented, skillful negotiators	**ESFP** Enthusiastic, innovative, tolerant, spontaneous, enjoy helping people	**ENFP** Versatile, optimistic, supportive, playful, enjoy starting new projects	**ENTP** Strategic, curious, challenging, outspoken, value inspiration
ESTJ Logical, conscientious, efficient, realistic, like to run the show	**ESFJ** Responsible, detailed, friendly, practical, enjoy being productive	**ENFJ** Congenial, loyal, verbal, diplomatic, skilled communicators	**ENTJ** Straightforward, strategic, independent, ambitious, effective organizer of people

The Myers Briggs Type Indicator(MBTI) comprises of100 questions which one answers to find out your personality type which is one of the above 16 Personality types.

But the problem is that people take the assessment and forget their type as it is very difficult to remember the 4 letters in your personality type.

It is time consuming as it is lengthy.

Also, MBTI does not tell you what to do next after you have learnt that you are of a certain personality type. So, is there a better way of learning about our strengths? And who we are as people? Yes! The DISC model.

The DISC Profiling Model

DISC is an acronym for the 4 Behavioral styles- Dominance, Influence, Steadiness and Compliance.

In the early 1920's, an American psychologist named William Moulton Marston developed a theory to explain people's emotional responses. He wanted to focus on the behavior of "normal" individuals(rather than the common focus of others on the mentally ill) and developed a four quadrant model based on Dominance, Influence, Steadiness and Compliance, the acronym being DISC.

Marston discovered that people do things for various reasons and are motivated by their reasons, not ours, and recognized that one individual could possess many traits, to more or less of a degree. It was the ***first time the four styles were identified as dynamic and situational*** which means the styles people displayed could change depending upon environmental factors and differing situations.

Marshton is also the person who invented the Lie Detector used till today successfully and also the creator of Wonder Woman.

The DISC model has continued to be researched and today is recognized as the most valid and reliable behavioral profiling tool to develop self-awareness. More than 50 million people worldwide from all differing contexts such as corporate leaders, industry professionals, managers, sales people, teachers, coaches and athletes have used DISC to improve their understanding of themselves and their behaviors. This is an assessment that is most popular today and easy to remember and understand. It has 24 questions that you answer, and takes about 10-15 minutes of your time.It is easy to remember because you know your major behavioral style is one of the four Dominance, Influence, Steadiness or Compliance. Each of these styles have their own motivators, demotivates, communication style, decision making style, relationship style etc. So, if you know your behavioral style, you know a lot about yourself.

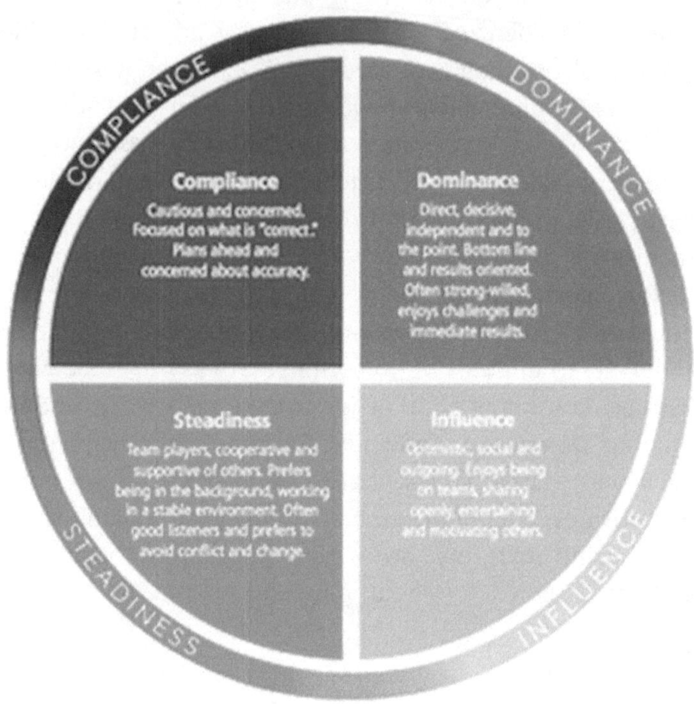

Extended DISC:

This is the most powerful DISC profiling tool that is available today. Extended DISC is extremely powerful as it measures the hard-wired DISC style and not what the respondent thinks and feels they should be. It measures the emotions of the respondents and tells us how the respondent is feeling. It is customizable and can be taken in multiple world languages.

You not only know your strengths, but also your weaknesses. You will know your communication style, your decision-making style, your leadership style. You know how you behave when you are paired with someone, how you will fare under stress, what kind of careers would you find the most natural rhythm and a whole lot more!

I recommend this assessment and personally have benefited a huge lot from it. If you want to take the assessment along with a debriefing, fill up the contact form on my website www.rinnkug.com and schedule a 15 minute conversation with me. This one decision of taking the Extended DISC assessment can bring about a huge paradigm shift in your life as it did in mine.

The Q9.

There are 9 questions that you need to answer and discover about yourselves to know who you really are. The above methods will give you insights into your personality.

The Q9 will be your personal success blueprint.

The Q9 are as below:

1. What are my personality traits?
2. What are my strengths?
3. What are my weaknesses or areas of improvement?
4. What is my communication style?
5. What is my decision making style?

6. What are my motivators or energisers?
7. What are my demotivators or de-energisers?
8. How do I work in a team or in a relationship?
9. What are my non-negotiable values?

Once you discover the answers to the above which I call the PERSONAL SUCCESS BLUEPRINT, you will be aware of your MOJO- your unique magical charm. We will learn what values are and why they are important in the next chapter.

Summary:

1. The study of human behavior is fascinating and has enamored scientists, psychologists and philosophers from centurie
2. We have various theories of human behavior across the centuries
3. Empedocles spoke about 'The Four Temperaments' . He said that the world is composed of four elements or, more precisely, 'roots' – fire, air, earth, and water.
4. Hippocrates propagated the 'Four Humor Theory' People were classified based on the fluids present in their body as Sanguine, Choleric, Melancholic or Phlegmatic.
5. The Zodiac Signs also speak about various personality traits based on the elements Air, Water, Earth and Fire
6. Ayurveda describes human personality or behavior based on the Tridoshas and Trigunas or the Prakriti-Guna combination.

7. The Myers-Briggs Type Indicator explains behavior based on the psychological types and there are 16 different personality types.
8. The DISC model- Based on Carl Jung's 4 behavioral axes represent 4 behavioral styles - Dominance, Influence, Steadiness and Compliance.
9. The Extended DISC model measures your emotions and how the person is feeling in addition to their dominant behavioral style
10. Your values are unique. It is important to discover Q9 to know your PERSONAL SUCCESS BLUEPRINT- your Mojo, your unique magical charm to obtain the results you wish to have in your life.

CHAPTER EIGHT

WHAT DRIVES YOU?

"What you drive and what drives you are inseparable; it defines your personality."

-Daniel Adudu Darlintine Uche

In the last chapter , we learnt about various models and theories that help us identify our behavioral traits. Each of those models helps in understanding a little bit more about ourselves. As human beings, we all have drivers or triggers that push us to do a certain action. Now, that action may have a good or a bad outcome. How do we change the outcomes then to make it something that we like or expect? Simple, we need to understand what our drivers are? What are those factors, situations, people, environment that drives you to do a certain thing well and to completely ruin another? Based on who you are as a person, your drivers change. We learnt that thoughts matter. Our beliefs, our inner dialogue matters. Our attitudes matter. All of these are our internal drivers. All of these put together are our VALUES.

VALUES are those things that drive us to do something.

Each of us has our own set of values and it completely depends on a whole lot of factors. Right from which country you come from, the geographical conditions like the weather, your family and friends, teachers, economic conditions, rituals and traditions you followed since childhood, what you observed and experienced while growing up and how you reacted to all of it.

Let's take the example of Jahan and Henna, two sisters who were orphaned in childhood. They lived in Delhi. They had no one to take care of them and started working in people's houses to feed themselves. One day, there was a visitor in Jahan's masters house. A lady who ran a NGO in Chennai came to visit them. Jahan who was 12 yrs old then, came in with a tray of tea and biscuits. The lady looked at her and asked her name and was surprised to hear Jahan responding in English. When she got to know that her parents were killed in a road accident and they had to leave school and start working, she offered to take them to Chennai and make them study. Jahan's master willingly let them go. Henna was 8 at that time. Both of them were put in a school in Chennai and looked after by the NGO.

While Jahan was very happy to have the opportunity to study and make something out of her life, Henna kept cribbing all the time. She hated the Chennai hot and humid weather, hated doing her chores at the NGO and grumbled that she was taken away from her home city.

Years later Jahan grew up to be a lawyer and Henna was struggling to complete her 12th std after failing.

Now, why am I narrating this story? Because the VALUES that each one had were very different. While Jahan valued 'Education' and believed that it would empower her, Henna did not value it. She kept focusing on how she was an orphan and how everyone around was just out to treat her badly or pity her.

VALUES are the foundations upon which we build a strong, successful and happy life. Here is an exercise that will help you identify your values.

EXERCISE

IDENTIFYING INNER VALUES & ASPIRATIONS

How are you showing up at work? In your personal relationships?

For yourself? How you show up in the world is determined by your core values.

It doesn't take years of self-reflection to uncover your core values. This simple exercise can help you determine them so you can start aligning your personal goals with them. How long will it take? About 10 minutes, well worth the investment!

Grab a pen and piece of paper and let's go!

1.1. Determine Your Core Values

From the list below, choose and write down every core value that resonates with you. Do not overthink your selection. As you read through the list, simply write down the words that feel like a core value to you personally. If you think of a value you possess that is not on the list, write it down.

Abundance
Acceptance
Accountability
Achievement
Adventure
Advocacy
Ambition
Appreciation
Attractiveness
Autonomy
Balance
Being the Best
Benevolence
Boldness
Brilliance
Calmness
Caring
Challenge
Charity
Cheerfulness
Cleverness
Collaboration
Community
Commitment
Compassion
Consistency
Contribution
Cooperation
Creativity
Credibility
Curiosity
Daring
Decisiveness
Dedication
Dependability
Diversity
Empathy
Encouragement
Enthusiasm
Ethics
Excellence
Expressiveness
Fairness
Family
Flexibility
Friendships
Freedom
Fun
Generosity
Grace
Growth
Happiness
Health
Honesty
Humility
Humor
Inclusiveness
Independence
Individuality
Innovation
Inspiration
Intelligence
Intuition
Joy
Kindness
Knowledge
Leadership
Learning
Love
Loyalty
Making a Difference
Mindfulness
Motivation
Optimism
Open-Mindedness
Originality
Passion
Performance
Personal Development
Peace
Perfection
Playfulness
Popularity
Power
Preparedness
Proactivity
Proactive
Professionalism
Punctuality
Quality
Recognition
Relationships
Reliability
Resilience
Resourcefulness
Responsibility
Responsiveness
Risk Taking
Safety
Security
Self-Control
Selflessness
Service
Simplicity
Spirituality
Stability
Success
Teamwork
Thankfulness
Thoughtfulness
Traditionalism
Trustworthiness
Understanding
Uniqueness
Usefulness
Versatility
Vision
Warmth
Wealth
Well-Being
Wisdom
Zeal

1.2. Group All Similar Values Together from the List of Values You Just Created

Group them in a way that makes sense to you, personally. Create a maximum of five groupings. If you have more than five groupings, drop the least important grouping(s). See the example below.

Abundance	Acceptance	Appreciation	Balance	Cheerfulness
Growth	Compassion	Encouragement	Health	Fun
Wealth	Inclusiveness	Thankfulness	Personal Development	Happiness
Security	Intuition	Thoughtfulness	Spirituality	Humor
Freedom	Kindness	Mindfulness	Well-being	Inspiration
Independence	Love			Joy
Flexibility	Making a Difference			Optimism
Peace	Open-Mindedness			Playfulness
	Trustworthiness			
	Relationships			

1.3. Choose One Word Within Each Group that Represents the Label for the Entire Group

Again, do not overthink your labels – there are no right or wrong answers. You are defining the answer that is right for you. See the example below – the label chosen for the grouping is bolded.

Abundance	Acceptance	Appreciation	Balance	Cheerfulness
Growth	Compassion	Encouragement	Health	Fun
Wealth	Inclusiveness	Thankfulness	Personal Development	**Happiness**
Security	Intuition	Thoughtfulness	Spirituality	Humor
Freedom	Kindness	**Mindfulness**	**Well-being**	Inspiration
Independence	Love			Joy
Flexibility	**Making a Difference**			Optimism
Peace	Open-Mindedness			Playfulness
	Trustworthiness			
	Relationships			

1.4. Add a Verb to Each Value Label

Add a verb to each value so you can see what it looks like as an actionable core value. For example:

- Live in freedom.
- Seek opportunities to make a difference.
- Act with mindfulness.
- Promote well-being.
- Multiply happiness.

This will guide you in the actions you need to take to feel like you are truly living on purpose.

1.5. Finally, Post Your Core Values Where You See Them when Faced with Decisions

Where should you post them? Write your core values in order of priority in your planner, so they are available as an easy reference when you are faced with decisions. Put them on a sticky note on the edge of your computer screen. Or make a background with them on it for your cell phone.

My Personal Core Values

Name: Rinnku. G
Date:

I am happy and grateful that I have identified my personal core values today. I shall keep these values visible always and will strive to live by them.

1. Live in Freedom
2. Seek opportunities for making a difference.
3. Act with mindfulness.
4. Promote well-being.
5. Multiply happiness.

1.6 Now Live Your Core Values!

If we can get to the place where we show up as our genuine selves and let each other see who we really are, the awe-inspiring ripple effect
will change the world-Terrie M. Williams

"Be the Change that you want to see in the world"-
Mahatma Gandhi

Summary:

1.The most important thing you can do for your personal success today is to know your core values and use them as your guide.

2. Knowing core values is important because when we need to choose or decide something, you can do so easily by simply determining if the choice lines up with your true core values.

3. A life lined-up with personal values is a well-lived, purpose-filled life.

4. Make sure you print your value card and keep it in a place where you can see it every day.

CHAPTER NINE

YOUR PERSONAL SUCCESS BLUEPRINT

"Knowing others is wisdom

Knowing Yourself is Enlightenment"

-Lao Tzu

In the last chapters we saw how values are our driving force in life.

Let's try to put together all that we discussed from the beginning to create your own unique Personal Success Blueprint. Your 'MOJO' The way I define MOJO is as below:

M-Me

O-Others

J-Joint Rhythm

O-Objectives & Key Results

So, there are 4 parts to finding your personal success blueprint, your MOJO.

THE FIRST PART- M-ME

Who you are determines what you achieve in life

Hence the journey of finding your MOJO begins with discovering yourself first. We learnt so far that there are 9 questions that you need to answer to unravel your **'ME'**

They are:

1. What are my personality traits?
2. What are my strengths?
3. What are my weaknesses or areas of improvement?
4. What is my communication style?
5. What is my decision making style?
6. What are my motivators or energisers?
7. What are my demotivators or de-energisers?
8. How do I work in a team or in a relationship?
9. What are my non-negotiable values?

Let me show you an example of how you can create your personal success blueprint by answering all the questions above.

Question 1: My Personality Traits

Pleasant, patient, empathetic,

Question 2: My Strengths

Peace loving and able to give and constructive feedback

Question 3: Weaknesses or areas of improvement

- Lose interest if there are too many details
- Cannot share disagreeing opinions, hence keep quiet and suffer

Question 4: My communication style

- Pleasant, people-oriented and good conversationalist
- Able to encourage and inspire people

- Can guide people

Question 5: My decision-making style

- Good, deliberate decision maker
- Will not analyze details too much, may use emotions to make decisions

Question 6: My motivators or energisers

- Good, encouraging and positive people around me
- Freedom to make my own decisions
- Open communication
- Ability to make a difference

Question 7: My demotivators or de-energisers

- Repetitive, monotonous routines
- Being isolated at work or in life
- No opportunity for team work
- Unemotional, cold people
- Being unpopular

Question 8: How do I work in a team or in a relationship?

- Suggest different alternatives
- Influence others to see the positive side
- Willing to listen to others views
- Open and sociable
- Make sure that others are comfortable

Question no 9: What are my non-negotiable values?

- Live in freedom.
- Seek opportunities for making a difference.
- Act with mindfulness.
- Promote well-being.
- Multiply happiness.

Now that completes the 'M' of the MOJO which is all about 'me'

THE SECOND PART-O-Others

Now the second part is the 'O' of the 'MOJO' which is all about others. Answer the Q9 for the person that you are looking at being in a relationship with. It is great if you can get the other person to complete the Q9 themselves. Whether that is a personal relationship or a work relationship, remember that people are different. What is your strength may not be theirs. You need to write down the answers to the Q9 by either speaking to that person directly or by noting down your observations from your experiences with the other person.

Now, a word of caution, write down only that which you have seen, heard, felt yourself. Do not go by what others have to say and what you have not experienced first-hand.

THE THIRD PART-J-JOINT RHYTHM

There is a story about the Parsis when they came to India. It is said that the king was worried about letting a new community settle down in the country. Sensing the king's hesitation, the leader of the Parsis asked for a glass of milk with sugar separately. When it was brought, he mixed the sugar in the milk and said " O king, you need not worry, we Parsis will blend in with your people just like the sugar in the milk. You need not worry at all" The king smiled and that's how the Parsis settled down in India.

Now, while this is how you would want all your relationships to be, to just blend in like sugar in milk and just become one. However, it is not always like this in reality. We don't always blend in so easily. We have to work towards obtaining a joint rhythm.

Even the sugar has to be stirred in the glass of milk so that it blends in.

Have you ever watched a dance performance or gone to a music concert? Each artist has to first master the art themselves then learn to synchronize and flow with the rest of the team. Only then will it be a bewitching performance, one that will enthrall the audience. If even one of the artists goes out of sync, then the performance is spoiled and it causes disappointment and becomes an eye-sore for the beholders and audience.

It takes self-awareness and deliberate action to obtain this joint rhythm. You would have to work on the relationship day after day. You would have to display understanding of not just the other person's behavior but learn to be patient and positive with yourself too. Be aware of complaining or cribbing about all the work that this is taking. If you do so, then it saps your energy and leaves you feeling exhausted. Think of it as unwrapping layers and layers of paper to discover the gift that you have been waiting for. Be excited about this process of exploring and discovering.

THE FOURTH PART-OF-Objectives & Key Results

You know your Q9 and you know the other person's Q9. Find out what is common, what are the shared interests between both of you. Also find out what are the shared vulnerabilities. And spend time talking about it. The more positive and patient conversations you have with each other, the better your relationship will become. You learn to recognise each other's triggers. You understand what is said and what is not said too. You learn to ignore the unimportant and work on what really matters. As long as you know what your end objectives are and what results you are looking at achieving together and you continue working on it, you will find your MOJO

As the saying goes " If you do not know where you want to go, then any road will do". So, you need to know what your end objectives and key results you seek are. Make sure that you enjoy the journey of reaching your destionation. Have fun and watch the sun rise, hear the birds chirp and enjoy your hot cup of tea. Life is all about the small joys. Don't wait to be happy. Be happy now.

Summary:

1. **Discover your MOJO**-Me,Others, Joint Rhythm and Objectives & Key Results
2. **M-Find your own Q9**- it will help you discover yourself
3. **O-Find the other person/team's Q9**-this will help you to know them better
4. **J- Joint Rhythm**-Work on the joint rhythm with them- just like a dancer must synchronize steps with the partner and enjoy the process.
5. **O-Define Objectives & Key Results**-Having defined objectives is important- find out shared interests, shared vulnerabilities, and shared goals.
6. Have conversations on what matters and agree to disregard the trivial matters.
7. Have fun along the way to achieving your objectives and be happy now.
8. The more you communicate with each other, the more you will learn about the other person or your team.
9. Have a mindset of trust and openness. Be optimistic about your progress and the change you want to see.

CHAPTER TEN

STAYING IN THE ZONE

Now that you have discovered your Mojo and have it all mapped up, the next thing to do is to find out what helps you '***Stay in the Zone***'. *Staying in the Zone* means that you are energetic, enthusiastic, and moving forward towards achievement of your goals, whether they are personal or professional and making progress day by day. It means that you get up and dust off your clothes and find the spirit to rise up and fight again every time you have a fall.

Life can be cruel and throw many challenges. It could be a sickness, loss of job, a heartbreak, the death of a loved one and so many other reasons to just give it all up and sigh. There's no one way to let go and go with the flow – what works for someone else may not work for you. We're all starting at different levels of perfectionism, control, mindful awareness, and more – try to be gentle with yourself as you navigate this process.

Here are 12 golden rules to 'Stay in the Zone'

1. **Stay in the present- practice mindfulness.**

There will be many situations that occur day in and day out that will give you frazzled nerves. There will be many events that will have you reacting in a manner that you regret later.

Most often, we say things or do things that we curse ourselves for later. While we don't mean to hurt others, the way we say it or do something might cause long term hurt and burn the bridges. Practicing mindfulness means that you become aware of how you react to every situation, to the triggers that bring out the best and the worst in you. It means that you become aware of all your emotions, happiness, sorrow, anger, guilt, fear, shame etc. Feel them all fully and reflect on why you are feeling that particular emotion. Is there any truth in what your mind is going on ranting about? Are you feeling helpless and feeling powerless? Are you losing control of yourself? When this happens, just go to a quiet spot, close your eyes, and just breathe in and breathe out. Let your mind chatter, let those thoughts come in and go, just don't let them linger for too long. You can also play one of the guided mindfulness meditations available now easily and freely on all music apps like iTunes, Spotify, Amazon music, YouTube etc

Take at least 5 minutes off to practice mindfulness. Do not judge yourself, belittle yourself while becoming aware of your thoughts or emotions. As you practice mindfulness meditation more and more, you will find that your responses to situations that trigger you become better. You will find yourself becoming calmer, having clarity of mind and being able to handle any situation in a much more effective manner.

2. Accept when things go out of your control

There is a circle of control that we all have. Some things are out of our control like the weather, market conditions, economic conditions of the country we live in etc. There is a saying that goes' Man proposes and God disposes' So, yeah God does have a funny way of reminding us of his/her presence. Not everything will go as you planned. The best thing to do is to accept when things go out of your control. Let it be. Maybe it was not meant to be. Maybe there is a better plan for you. Accept that whatever happens is for your greater good. I say the below prayer every time I find things going out of my control.

> ***'God grant me the serenity to accept the things I cannot change, the courage to change the things I can and the wisdom to know the difference.'***

Print the above prayer on a piece of paper and stick it on your bathroom mirror, your cupboard, save it as your phone wallpaper, anywhere you can see it every day. It has helped me a lot in going with the flow and accepting things and I am sure it will help you too.

3. Change your intention-Get into a flow state

In psychology, "flow" is a state of mind in which you're so immersed in whatever you're doing that you forget about the world around you. You're "in the zone" in the best way. You're not self-conscious. You're not even having any thoughts about what you're doing. You're simply doing it.

The concept of a "flow" state was first named by positive psychology researcher Mikaly Csikszentmihalyi. He wrote that our "*best moments*" usually occur when a person's body or mind is stretched to its limits in a voluntary effort to accomplish something difficult and worthwhile."

To intentionally enter a flow state, choose an activity that's meaningful to you. It shouldn't be so easy that you feel bored, nor so difficult that you feel frustrated. The more you enter a "flow" state, the more you'll be immersed in the present. This could mean spending some time at the gym working out, taking time out for a walk in the park, working on that difficult assignment, taking time out to talk to a person that you wanted to catch up in a long time, writing that poem/article that you wanted to, designing something creative etc. Any activity that is meaningful for you and creates joy and a feeling of accomplishment will get you in a state of flow.

4. Stay Flexible with your schedule

One key piece to going with the flow is not to maintain too rigid of a schedule. Planning and setting goals for the future is healthy, and beneficial for your mental health.

At the same time, if you're too strict with your plans, it may prevent you from going with the flow when circumstances change.

Continue setting short- and long-term goals. But keep in mind that not everything is within your control. When outside circumstances, which are out of your control, interrupt these plans, try not to let them derail you completely. It may help to focus on your next steps and change strategies.

5. Practice self-compassion and self-love

Sometimes, it becomes difficult to go with the flow because we're so hung up on punishing ourselves for mistakes. When you can't let go of the mistakes you've made, it can be hard to move on or to stay in the moment.

According to Dr. Kristin Neff's research from 2022, you can practice self-compassion by first understanding that making mistakes (and feeling bad about them) connects you to all of humanity; everyone makes mistakes.

Then, accept how you're feeling with no judgment; simply sit with it without becoming attached. Lastly, be kind to yourself and intentionally speak to yourself as if you would to a dear friend.

6. Use your breath

Sometimes, we can lose track of the present because we get lost in our thoughts. One way to balance this is by returning to the present moment using your breath.

Many mindfulness teachers use the breath as a guiding anchor through meditation. But you don't need to be seated on a meditation cushion for your breath to be able to help you.

When you find yourself getting lost in thoughts about the past or the future, simply bring your attention to your breathing. You can always use your breath to return to the moment.

7. Accept your feelings

Typically, when people feel emotional pain, they want to push it away. However, when you push down feelings in this way, they can come back to haunt you. Instead of pushing painful feelings down, try to accept them.

For example, you may have planned an outdoor wedding only for a big storm to roll in on that day. It's positive to be able to go with the flow, accept that the weather is out of your control, and make new plans.

At the same time, you probably have feelings of disappointment – and it's healthy to accept those feelings, too. Your feelings are valid. You can accept your disappointment as well as the fact that the weather is out of your control.

8. Remember to play

Learning not to take yourself too seriously can go a long way in helping you go with the flow more. Find opportunities to play and be silly.

One great way to incorporate play into your life is by laughing more. A 2019 literature review found that laughter has many mental health benefits, including:

- increasing positive emotion
- reducing stress
- improving relationships

9. Let go of perfection

Perfectionism is a common personality trait. Although it can have advantages, it can also have consequences when it's maladaptive. Unfortunately, dysfunctional types of perfectionism have become more common, especially in young people.

Instead of focusing on being perfect, focus on striving for excellence. Unlike perfectionism, people who strive for excellence don't need things to be perfect – they simply have high standards that they strive to meet.

Having the understanding that you don't need to be perfect to be excellent may help you to stay in the flow and learn to let go.

10. Reexamine your values

Make sure that your goals still align with your values. Sometimes, people set long-term goals and work tirelessly to achieve them. But values can change with time. Do the goals that you set long ago still reflect your values today?

Don't be afraid to change your goals if they no longer align with your values and beliefs. This is part of going with the flow. Strictly following previous goals, without reexamining them, isn't likely to bring you any happiness or fulfillment.

11. Be aware of daily fluctuations

There may be times during the day or week when you're more easily able to find your "flow," and other days when it's more difficult. Be aware of these fluctuations in energy levels and focus.

Take advantage of the days it's easier to find your flow. But also be aware of factors that could be making you more rigid or stressed. Have you gotten enough sleep? Have you been eating well? How are your relationships?

12. Get support

Lastly, if you're finding it very difficult to go with the flow and let go of control in your life, then you could benefit from working with a mental health therapist.

Therapists aren't only for people with diagnosable mental illnesses; they can help you learn how to stay in the moment and become more flexible in your thinking.

Summary:

1. Stay in the present- practice mindfulness.
2. Accept when things go out of control
3. Change your intention-Get into a flow state
4. Stay flexible with your schedule
5. Practice self-compassion and self-love

6. Use your breath
7. Accept your feelings
8. Remember to play
9. Let go of perfection
10. Re-examine your values
11. Be aware of daily fluctuations
12. Get support

CHAPTER ELEVEN

LOVE YOUR LIFE

Loving your life involves cultivating a positive mindset, engaging in fulfilling activities, and taking care of your physical and emotional well-being.

Here are some things you can do to enhance your love for life:

Practice Gratitude: Regularly reflect on the things you're grateful for. This can shift your focus from what's lacking to what you already have. I heard this quote when I was a child and it has left a deep imprint on my mind since then

"I cried because I had no shoes until I met a man who had no feet." — Helen Keller

There are so many thing that we should be grateful for in our lives.

The air we breathe that helps us be alive, the food we eat that nourishes and energises us, the water we drink that is the life force without which we cannot survive, the roof on our head and the clothes we wear that protect us from the vagaries of the heat, dust, rain and harsh winters. Our parents who are there for us always supporting us and doing everything they can to keep us happy. Our siblings who share our joys and sorrows. Our friends who are there for us with a listening ear, every time we want to share something, our teachers and mentors who guide us and help us achieve our life goals. A smiling child, a helpful neighbour, the numerous people like tailors, doctors, maids, cooks, drivers, the online delivery people who bring our groceries and other essentials to our doorstep, these are all examples of so many examples of blessings in our life.

We will be able to find so many blessings around us if we look carefully.

Make it a practice to maintain a Gratitude Journal and write down at least 5 things that you are grateful for every day before you sleep at night. You will slowly start attracting all the best things in your life. A grateful heart is positive, humble and joyful. There is no place for anything negative when you are being thankful for something or to someone.

Connect with Others: Build and nurture relationships with family, friends, and social groups. Positive social interactions can significantly contribute to your happiness.

Engage in Activities You Enjoy: Pursue hobbies and activities that bring you joy. Whether it's reading, painting, playing a musical instrument, or hiking, engaging in things you love can boost your mood.

Practice Self-Care: Take care of your physical and mental well-being. Eat nutritious foods, exercise regularly, get enough sleep, and manage stress effectively.

Help Others: Acts of kindness and helping others can create a sense of fulfillment and purpose. Volunteer or contribute to your community in meaningful ways.

Celebrate Achievements: Acknowledge your accomplishments, both big and small. Celebrating your successes can boost your self-esteem and overall happiness.

Embrace Change: Life is full of changes. Instead of fearing them, try to embrace change as an opportunity for growth and new experiences.

Practice Positive Self-Talk: Challenge negative thoughts and practice self-compassion. Treat yourself with the same kindness you would offer to a friend.

Limit Comparison: Avoid excessive comparison with others, especially through social media. Focus on your journey and progress, rather than comparing yourself to others.

Spend Time in Nature: Spending time outdoors and enjoying nature can have a calming and rejuvenating effect on your mind and spirit.

Cultivate Resilience: Life has its ups and downs. Developing resilience can help you navigate challenges with a positive attitude and bounce back from setbacks.

Laugh and Have Fun: Incorporate humor and playfulness into your life. Laughter is a powerful tool for boosting your mood and reducing stress.

Learn, Grow and Reach for the Stars: Continue learning and seeking personal development. This can be through formal education, reading, online courses, or attending workshops. Learning is a lifetime activity. There is no age to learn something new. When you stop learning, you stop growing in life. So, keep learning, growing and reaching for the stars! Remember that loving your life is a journey, and it takes time and effort.

Be patient with yourself and allow yourself to explore different activities and strategies to find what resonates most with you.

Summary:

1. An attitude of gratitude is the foundation of a happy, successful life

2. Connecting with people helps nurture relationships

3. Be kind and help others

4. Celebrate all your wins however tiny they may be

5. Change is the only constant in life. Embrace it.

6. You are your best cheerleader. Practice positive self-talk.

7. Do not compare your life with others

8. Nature is the best healer. Spend time in nature.

9. Be resilient. Bounce back everytime.

10. Laughter is the best medicine

11. Never stop learning.

12. You are unique! Your Mojo, your unique magical charm is what is required for your success!

Sources

https://www.scientificamerican.com/article/how-your-brain-is-wired-reveals-the-real-you/

https://www.psychologynoteshq.com/psychological-field-theory/

https://www.simplypsychology.org/naturevsnurture.html

https://www.verywellmind.com/attitudes-how-they-form-change-shape-behavior-2795897

https://www.ncbi.nlm.nih.gov/pmc/articles/PMC3215408/

https://ayurvedichospital.com/en-blog/demystifying-doshas-vata-pitta-kapha

https://www.ncbi.nlm.nih.gov/pmc/articles/PMC3830173/

https://www.annualreviews.org/doi/abs/10.1146/annurev-psych-032420-031047

https://journals.sagepub.com/doi/full/10.1177/0734282919881928

https://ejournal.lucp.net/index.php/mjn/article/view/laughter

https://psycnet.apa.org/record/2022-34332-001

About The Author

Rinnku is on a mission to help 100,000 people achieve financial independence, success and happiness using Identity Coaching. She helps people 'Discover their Mojo', their unique blueprint to success using a mix of behavioral profiling tools, people development interventions and occult sciences. She is the founder of Rightwaay Talent Consulting and Motley Mentors, State President of WICCI Mentoring & Soft skills council, HR

Mentor, Numerologist, Vastu Consultant and a published author. She has won awards like 'Iconic Women Creating a Better World for All' at the WEF and 'South India's 50 Most Talented HR Leaders' at the Asia HRM Congress. She is the founder of the Nakshatra Tribe, which is a strong community of people helping each other to Learn, Grow and Reach for the Stars! Her desire is to spread the wave of positivity and empower and touch as many lives as she can in her lifetime. She loves writing in Hindi and English and her poems have been published in multiple anthologies and holds a certificate of publication by the World Book of Records, London.

Follow the author on *http://www.instagram.com/rinnkug*

For personalised coaching sessions, email *info@rinnkug.com* or contact on the website *www.rinnkug.com*

www.ingramcontent.com/pod-product-compliance
Lightning Source LLC
La Vergne TN
LVHW091117150826
845673LV00002B/874